Playground

By Joe Benevento

Playground

By Joe Benevento

Published by Unsolicited Press
www.unsolicitedpress.com

Cover Art: Kathryn Gerhardt
Editor: S.R. Stewart

For information, contact the publisher at info@unsolicitedpress.com

Unsolicited Press Books are distributed to the trade by Ingram.
Printed in the United States of America.
ISBN: 978-1-947021-97-6

Table of Contents

After Zoraida Martínez Saved Me from Divine Word Seminary

I was an annoyingly religious and self-righteous sort,
never cursing, like almost all the other boys, certain,
at age eleven I wanted to become a religious, a brother
at that, since part of my early arrogance was to proclaim myself unworthy
of standing in for Jesus as a priest.

So extreme my own mother, conspiring with the Sisters
of Saint Joseph, rulers of Saint Teresa of Avila school,
tried to forbid my plan for leaving home
to start a seminary life age thirteen in Pennsylvania
with the Divine Word Order. I was certain I lived

that Word too fully to let them block my way.
Then the Martinezes moved in five doors down;
three daughters ages 12-16, capturing multiple
pretenders, none of whom saw Holy Joey a rival,
though the youngest, Zoraida, a name retrieved

from the madness of *Don Quixote*- her topaz eyes
favored me. First she sent pebbles my direction
which only my best friend José interpreted as a sign, next
she confessed to my little brother who it was
she had chosen, so that even I could not forestall

the necessary revelation, our hand-holding sending
golden, electric shocks through me like nothing
praying had ever produced, taking me away from my Divine
Word pretension to admitting my weakness, like a budding
cherry blossom admits the sun, knowing all my poetry would come

from then on as a way to be always recalling that miracle.

Stay-at-Home Dad

My father missed World War II;
a perforated eardrum kept him
in Canarsie, instead of Normandy
Iwo Jima or Khartoum.

Later, poverty plus seven
children never allowed him west
of Jersey till he was past 50
and our Greyhound trek to Tulsa relatives.

A little later still he went to Florida,
but not to snorkel or fish for tarpon,
just furniture lifting, to bring my sister
back after years away from Long Island.

He'd get to Ohio and Michigan to see
my graduations, small town Missouri
to witness my second wedding, but
never anywhere just for him.

By the time he could retire from
his maintenance man job he was 73;
Mom was too sick to travel
and he'd not go anywhere without her.

So, aside from an occasional
bus trek with the other seniors
to lose some quarters in Atlantic City,
he's been stuck in working-class Queens.

He never will get to Colonial Williamsburg (history buff)
Calabria (where his parents were born) nor even
Chicago. At 89, cane-reliant diabetic, my poor
father, after life's long labor, stays at home,

though he's with me
everywhere I go.

Break-In

"No viste entre sueños
por e aire vagar una sombra
ni sintieron tus labios un beso
que estalló misterioso el la alcoba?

-Gustavo Adolfo Bécquer

In this dream of you we are talking
politely; there are others around.
In this dream I am wishing you would
want me, looking at your face reminds
me of love, though you rarely smile.
Suddenly I awake to the bedroom
door slamming. I see only my fear,
my heart pounds:
"Who's there?" your image quickens
to assure, "I've come for you," and my fear
mixes with the shock of longing
your breaking entrance brings.
As I see you slip into my bed, I awake
again to a room without you, wishing
the dream had lasted longer, wondering
if I can ever awaken again
without searching for you
in the surreal shadows
of supposed daylight.

Birthday Present

You go up the long, red staircase to your
apartment, her legs first flashing
in front of her blue denim skirt. Passing
her to insert the key, you enter, get her
some burgundy, yourself a beer.
On the blue couch Anita Baker sings
of mystery and rapture as if sensing
the emeralds hanging from her ears,
making up her eyes.

She presents a hypothetical case:
some spoken-for woman you wanted, wanted
you; the wine shaking in the glass,
the beer still in the unopened bottle.
She edges closer to tell you
about the man who is making her crazy,
not you, yet she heats the room
with what-ifs anyway because she wants you
to sigh absolution, annul your hard-
earned reputation for fidelity, you,
the man who can take her to dinner, bring
her home and never quiver: now it isn't only
the wine shaking. You get up to go
to the bathroom, change the tape
to some easy listening music, put her
empty glass in the sink, bring back
some ice water.

Loser

"Battles are lost in the same spirit in which they are won."
                                        -Walt Whitman, "Song of Myself"

The qualities of loss often conceal
how winning is a limit and a lie,
since human nature would much rather deal
with touchdown dances than with kids who cry
their disbelief we just want them to try
their best. They know better, they know too well
winning gets parades, applause, proud eyes
that say well done, instead of damn it, hell,
how did you miss that pitch, that pass, oh, well,
we'll practice more, or send you to a camp,
some place where they do all they can to sell
you on the notion that there's just one stamp,
one way to court the dark drug of winning,
to hide how life is loss from the beginning.

After I Was Selected for the St. John's University Summer Track Program for Disadvantaged Youth

I walked five blocks the wrong way to get the right
 bus to take us all to campus, my only white face
in a vehicle full of brothers in poverty and race
running prowess, though my many cross
country medals meant almost nothing

once we got to the track where
I was the most overmatched
not only in foot speed but endurance
of guys I hadn't grown up with, a few of whom
enjoyed tormenting the cracker with insults, or petty

thefts of my sandwich (they gave us poor boys lunch)
or soda money from the locker I could not afford to lock,
its combination too befuddling, every aspect
of my days there exhausting, confusing, since
I had imagined it was all going to be good,

a reward for running around the block multiple
times, turning 130th Street into a track where
there was none, and so earning my chance to train
with experts. But none of the coaches could solve my
missteps; all I ended up with was a terrible cough kicking

into months-lasting bronchitis, a definitive destruction
of my dopey Olympic dream, an understanding
of why the one guy on the bus back who looked out
for me some actually turned my disoriented self around
one early evening when I false-started his way,

pointing instead towards the proper lane to distance myself from them all.

Marilyn Meshak

"In dreams, I walk with you.
In dreams, I talk to you."
                    -Roy Orbison

Taunted by the pale blue
ice of her eyes, in a photo
from forty years before,
I sit remembering Marilyn Meshak,
and all the times I told her
of my love, alone, in my bedroom,
or roaming the unsafe streets
of Queens, wishing
to do what I never did,
and never dids are hard to dissolve,
no matter how I finally got unshied enough
to date, marry, divorce, marry again,
bring children, brown and green-eyed
into the same unflinching world.
Somehow that first, ongoing failure
has nailed me, if not as loser
certainly as lost, dreaming dozens
of dreams each year since of conversations,
kisses, connection to a petite blonde phantom.

Maybe she lives like me an anonymous life,
maybe she died young and is all the more my ghost,
either way, we are as far from our days
sharing a school building, a bus stop,
a neighborhood as it's possible to be,
more time past only making my dreams more
redundant, pained, to wake up and uncover
how I'll never tell her

what I felt, and, so, still feel,
how I'll never know her, and, so
somehow making everyone unknowable,
unreachable, whether awake, alone
or, finally,
asleep together.

After Singing All Night for Twenty Bucks and a Bagel

I walked, cased guitar in hand, smoke releasing itself
from my clothes into the N. High Street air, its October
chill lengthening out a little past midnight, with hints
of future snow. I had shared about everything I knew
at Bernie's Bagels: three sets of fifteen songs each

to people way more concerned with whether their beers
went better with the Reuben or the poppy seed tuna bagel
than with how well I was covering Dylan
or Stevens or, my particular favorite, Ian Anderson,
his "Cross Eyed Mary" only my most obvious

attempt not to settle for being background music
for boozy strangers. I even mixed in a few of my own
compositions, still not completely resigned
to admitting my hope of becoming a famous singer-
songwriter was blackened toast, scraping together

as I had this repertoire of melodies to merit
a regular spot on Bernie's schedule, though not
even I could conjure a dream where I'd believe I
could be discovered while laboring in the smoky darkness
of a windowless bar-bagel shop in a basement

in Columbus, Ohio, where I was a graduate student as
indifferent to my studies as the customers had been to my
singing, not so bad as to call attention to itself, but not good
enough to matter. Even my guitar case smelled
of my defeat, though I knew the odor would not linger long

enough to prevent me from stringing myself a little longer.

Dancing with a Dutch Girl

The way she worked her loose blue
dress was most like a lethal weapon
with the safety on, for now.
She was all grace, smile, accented
sophistication, control, even
as she downed light
beers, even as she smoked my
air with cigarettes she had
personally rolled.
I can't imagine anyone more
beguiling, indulging
herself on those too rare
occasions the loud, lousy band
would break and at least
danceable canned music
would elevate us away
from the disappointment
of having nothing surprising
to say.

Her blue-green eyes danced almost
as much as her toes; her spins and jumps
made me aware of how night
prances back to day
and even the most alluring
of partners will hang you
over the truth of your joy-
less life, make you desire
a return to a time when you sought
to hold someone's gaze in the shadow
of your embrace, for no other
motive than love.

April 26th

"In the day, in the night, to all, to each,
Sooner or later delicate death."
                    -Walt Whitman, "When Lilacs Last In The Dooryard Bloom'd."

Worms were all over the wet street,
as I walked my eleven-year-old Schnauzer
the morning of my father's 91st birthday.
Often I'll collect them in my not-leash-holding hand,
feel them squirming with the life I'll grant
in an earthy container in the refrigerator,
only to find themselves, in a few days
dangling bait for fish my son and I will catch
and release.

This morning, though, derailed by the near
certainty Dad will never see ninety-two,
his heart having become, like all things, finally, unreliable,
I can't be responsible for any life
and death decisions, so leave the worms
lurching in the street, where soon some
will meet the fate of their already dismembered cousins,
assaulted by mini-van or hungry robin. I think
instead of how few years the dog has left,
my own questionable heart, and whether it will keep
working nearly as long as my father's has.

As I drive to work, I listen to Frank Sinatra's voice
preserved on CD, an often unholy man blessed
in finding a way to seek sympathy past
his body's finale, the sure melody he prays
"Time After Time," reminding me of the only thing
worth any worry, "so lucky to be loving you,"
and a tear trickles down for my dad, my dog,

myself, even for the worms I may be running over,
making me wish I had accepted the mess the mass
of them in one wet hand would have been, to take them
not to cold storage, but a gentle return to their own dirt,
to spend at least a few not fully futile hours more
in this sad miracle no one still whole
should ever be asking to exit.

After Driving to See Sylvia in Nebraska

where she and her folks were visiting her brother José, choosing
to spend the Christmas holidays in freezing Fremont, instead
of Fajardo, Puerto Rico, where Sylvia had been staying
since the Ramos family split Queens fifteen years before.
Already having failed, by age 31, at three marriages,

Sylvia waited until early January to find me still trying
to fail my first, as I fled too busy Carmen, risking
the snowy road, the can't go home again injunction
that might encompass being unable to rekindle
all that unrequited fire, so many winters passing.

Sylvia Ramos was unchanged, the same
mixture of beguiling beauty tempered by modesty
unmolested by the hands of time or men.
We could still pretend there was only friendship
between us, that my Cuban wife back in Kirksville

was glad I was getting to revisit the Ramoses,
that my now full fluency in Spanish could bring
us no closer than the space between seats
in the front of my mistrusty old Pinto,
as I drove Sylvia Ramos to the Omaha airport,

her two year old sleeping in the back,
the rest of the Ramoses in José's van, so Sylvia
could soft talk away all the years, convince me
how right I was to keep believing
in her, how nice I was so ready to remain

the faithful knight to her maddening Dulcinea.

Unsettled

"People wish to be settled: only so far as they are unsettled is there any
hope for them."

-Emerson, "Circles"

Even hope can be carried too far:
cull it away from its sources and it
starts to taste like desperation,
like the guy who is an agnostic, but only
for lack of something better to believe
that would not call for so much faith,
someone with a good job, but a consistent
desire to find a better one,
a house people say they admire
but which whispers sinister sounds
at him from pipes, paint, the very foundation
shifting, still somehow not settled
after seventeen years.
He still has his parents, but they cannot
live forever, still plays basketball, but
on questionable knees, has young
children, but never underestimates
the odds of disease, accident, or, at least
the predicted contempt of their teenaged years.
To the adage about fear itself remaining
the only thing to fear he might respond:
"I was afraid that was true,"
only pretending to joke, sensing
his only real hope held in how
adroitly he can feign tranquility
in the face of all he hopes will not
befall him
each unsettling day.

After December 25th

A student or teacher all but five
years of my ten times five life,
I've never suffered the necessity of work
the next morning. I can stay home with the kids
navigating a sloppy sea of strewn toys,

tables covered with gifts we haven't figured
a place for, a too quickly withering poinsettia,
the impetus of regret
tied to an empty
container of eggnog.

Christian clergy tell us to carry Christmas
past the 25th, into all of winter still to come,
but how many believe we'll try? Right now
the tree still holds every ornament: each candy cane,
golden ball, shining star a sign

we hang hopes ever
green with the thought there is
something more lasting
than once pretty paper torn
towards the garbage,

the tree itself,
an early New Year's orphan
on the roadside,
no room in the in-
side of these littered homes

until next December.

What Cannot Be Feigned

"I like a look of agony,"

—Emily Dickinson

Emily says you just can't do it-
fake a death throe, convince any mammal
really paying attention that you're gone
when you aren't, which is why we call it
playing possum, and, really, she was right.

The many dead marsupials I've seen
in my life wending its way
on woodsy roads in Michigan or Missouri
have always ended with a look
too true to be faked,

a countenance locked in grim surprise
those lights could get to them so fast,
carrying something so final.
Even when there is no blood
scarletting the street

even when all the important injuries
are internal, as in life,
that perfectly possum body
surely will not rise again,
there being, after all,

so much more to dying than lying
perfectly still, suffering
a few flies to ponder future
maggot nurseries
on your quiet corpus.

Not Fishing with Jim

"Rainbow flies dance and dip before us;
daylight fades, pink and orange.

-Joe Benevento, "Fishing With Jim" Holding On

Jim, they now stock trout in Kirksville, rainbows
splash in Spur Pond, starting each November.
Joey and I went Tuesday, had the place
just to ourselves, caught ten fish between
us, hooked a dozen more that jumped so much
they shook free. Jim, there isn't a day goes
by I don't think of you. Do you remember
all the bass I caught, the shock on your face
when they preferred my fake worm to those keen,
artful flies you fashioned yourself? How much
I regret how you fled this town for trout
fishing closer to home, and now you've left
me twice over, since death leaves you without
visiting rights, and me lure-less, bereft.

Miami Night with Marjorie and Todd

I'm not sure I really believe
I'm eating alligator at the tapas bar,
but who cares? The semi-tropical evening
has just begun its descent, a female mariachi trio
are stroll-singing "Solamente Una Vez,"
only my favorite song, and this perfect couple
of friends, who met years earlier in my American
Romanticism class are ready to share with me all
they have figured out so far about southern Florida.

Ironically, I fled a Cuban up in Connecticut
to get here, a short break from a long bad marriage,
to practice my Spanish some place
where it will be better appreciated.
Just these first hours I'm substituting for snow
with a moist, white "tres leches" cake at a Cuban café,
freeing myself up with a few Cuba libre at an elegant bar,
becoming intoxicated with the almost full moon over Miami
as a suspension of my disbelief in the magical
realness of my future possibilities, from this city
with too much music, friendship and night
life for me to insist any longer
on my regret.

No Competition

I worried whether my son would be jealous
when I asked my eldest, Maria, 10, to draw
some butterflies for the cover
of my book of poems.

The publisher got the idea from my "Recycling"
about Maria, at 3, drawing and coloring
on the flip side of some of my
rejected manuscripts.

But, Joey, who doesn't draw often,
he's our insect expert. And butterflies
are bugs, no matter how pretty their wings, how much
they might epitomize metamorphosis.

When I get home, I see Joey has made
as many butterflies as Maria,
I tell him maybe they can both send samples
to my publisher; it's a small press.

But Joey says, no, that's okay, he wants to keep all
he has created. He gets kid scissors, cuts them out,
puts a bit of tape on each of their backs, decorates the wall
behind his bed with their multicolored happiness.

If there's a flaw in each child's
depictions, it's how cute
and friendly they have made
their butterflies' faces.

Look close enough at a real one's head
and you'll see the part that's still caterpillar
ugly.

But it's a child's drawings we wanted for
the book, for the bedroom,
for as long as possible.

Playground

I could tell my spouse disapproved
of the blonde in short-shorts, sitting
on the sidewalk with a cell-phone,
her toddler tipping a Pepsi,
time and again into her dirty mouth.
Our clean sixteen-month old, Claire
was safely in her stroller, with milk
to drink if she wanted something wet.
The other mother scored no points
by speaking with us; whatever
she might have gained by letting us learn
she worked rather than welfared, offset
by the pack of Marlboros she chose
from while she chatted.

I cannot pretend secondary smoke seems
good for a small child, but I am less inclined
than usual to judge, remembering five minutes before,
when my wife was yelling at our five year old,
whose blood was only a little diluted by his tears.
Anyone encountering us for the first time
would have no way of knowing we never hit
him, his bleeding caused by narrow nasal passages,
nor would they suppose the patient, loving
parent his mother almost always is.
So when Carol complains in the car
about the faulty parenting we have just witnessed,
I recall instead the constant, happy smile
of the defendant's daughter, am willing to assume
it evidence of the quality of a mother's love,
the tar and nicotine, sugar and caffeine
notwithstanding.

"I'm never going to dream of fairies"

...my four-year-old Margaret laments,
a bit after I make the mistake of pretending
I purchased her fairy-book-birthday-present
from an actual fairy store.
She petitioned to have me take her
to that magic place the next time
any of us needed a fairy item, but when I tried
to sidetrack that goal, she wondered how she would
ever really get to meet a fairy,

her lit up hope already flickering, like Tinkerbelle
before we clapped her all the way back to life.
It only got worse when I admitted
the fairy store was only pretend,
suggested the best place to meet
a fairy was in her dreams.
She was certain she'd never get that lucky,
though I reminded her just a week before
she'd assured me I'd never catch her a fish

and not five minutes later I had
a glowing rainbow
trout for her to pet lightly and release.
"But fish are different," she almost cried
and she knew I knew the difference
and was powerless to pretend any further
that I didn't. Her sleep that night was fitful,
all her dreams just silly
she said when she awoke.

After Math

I was an arithmetic whiz at 4&1/2,
adding and subtracting quicker than my 6
year old sister. But from long division on I faltered,
struggled, hated my many ways through all the proofs,
charts and problems of my life through 12th grade.

I ended up at NYU in part to avoid Columbia's
math requirement, acing myself out of the Ivy League
just to never not excel again the way I always could
in literature, languages, music, philosophy;
rustiness in trigonometry for the GRE's probably costing me

Ivy League again, so I settled for the Big 10
for graduate school. Many years later, my 4 children
all do very well in math, but none of them like it,
not even Claire, invited in the 7th to skip to
8th grade algebra 1, nor my son Joey who had

a 30 on his practice ACT. For the reading part
he earned a perfect 36. I'm figuring if he had done
the reverse, he would have kept it from me, knowing as he
has since about age 4, I agree with fiction's Dupin in "The
Purloined Letter: algebra is very overrated.

And so, my 4 children all have or will get ACT composite
scores around 33, and most likely be denied the Ivy too,
settling for something not quite as standardly stellar,
like my eldest, Maria, newly in the Honors Program at Creighton,
which she chose in part to bypass any core math requirements, so she 2

can try to ignore the tyranny of #'s, B just like her Dad.

After Realizing I Didn't Have Enough Money

to send my eldest of four to a private college
unless she got close to a "full ride," I was comforted
knowing my teaching at this almost
first rate "public ivy" assured all my children
seventy-five per cent off their college educations,

but when it became clear Maria
wasn't going to be happy going to her father's
U., staying in the same small town near to nothing
where she has spent her first eighteen years listening
to my nostalgia for a larger world, I talked my wife into

an overestimation of our solvency, saying we could
afford to throw ten grand a year toward Maria's
hopes. My daughter's a lot happier, maybe
it's even a better school, though probably
only in ways a lot less measurable

than forty-g's. And her brother starts
college in a year and a half already
assuming he should go someplace special too,
while my wife, well, I promised her long ago
she'd never have to work outside

the home unless she wanted to, which she does
not, so, I'm wishing I was bankrupt
enough to become an administrator,
or foolish enough to believe in the lottery,
some other magic means to protect my long

cherished claim money doesn't matter.

After Finding Those Cavalcanti Poems

in their "dolce stil nuovo" now eight hundred years
old, but still there for the seeking out in cyberspace,
unlike when I first met them, in an old book at the new NYU library,
part of my Italian homework for a report
I turned into an excuse for singing, setting them to music

nothing like what they had in 13th century Florence,
though I felt Guido's lament over the loved one's
unassailable power over her victim at least as much
as he had, no matter how more skilled
his words than my music.

Those solo days I sought out masters
of the unrequited, from Catullus to Bécquer
to Keats, set their sorrow to my minor guitar chords
and intent baritone, shared the results with encouraging
classmates, disconcerting belles dames sans merci.

I kept those songs close to me long past
college, years after I'd found someone
to requite me, discovering too late the sweeter,
sharper stay in loss, the pregnant power in longing
lasting longer than any love making could.

Now, having forgotten too many of the words, I seek
them out anew, so I can match them once more to my
melodies, share them with my teenagers who love
to sing, who bring their own new styles to long dead
Keats, to Cavalcanti, to all our almost lost love

songs, which only their young voices can revive.

Lemon-Blueberry Cake

Adding a half cup of lemon
curd, lemon extract replacing
vanilla, plus one pint of blue-
berries, turned Betty Crocker's
cookbook concept of a yellow cake
to a dessert dense with optimism
topped with buttercream
frosting rescued from regular
by a quarter cup more curd.

To think how delivered I myself felt
from failure's embrace after seeing
the cake's center pockmarked
with bubbles seven minutes before
completion, instead settling for faith,
leaving the cake's chemistry to answer
for its additions, seeing, once out, how
the fresh fruit had volunteered itself
to the bottom of the pan, tart taste
throughout, and, once cooled, sealed
in yellow-white waves of citrus sweetness.

Something new to share with company
coming from far away, lightening the day
sunshine yellow, as all real gratitude
can do, a creation which you too now share,
should you choose to unravel the recipe
of that almost perfect poem.

Bonifacio Payaso

is the name I gave to the paper clown
my seven-year-old created, colored
and cut out as one character
for an elaborate game she trusted
I would play with her.

She gave her cut-out characters fronts
and backs, suggested the protagonists
be the clown and a princess-ballerina
we gave my daughter's own name,
Margaret, with whom the clown
would of necessity fall in love.

I made-up for my multi-colored hero the silliest
name I could conjure, Bonifacio Payaso,
payaso the noun for clown in Spanish,
Bonifacio a name exotic to Margaret
and surely worth a chuckle from her
three much older siblings.

Still, as the game progressed,
the two of us acting out
the many characters created,
the plaintive, trusting way Princess Margaret
would say Bonifacio's name, he who had promised
to save her from the evil prince (involving magic
juggling balls, a force field and a lot of faith)

made me happy and hurt simultaneously:
glad to have a seven-year-old capable
of recognizing back to love even
the silliest sounding of my offerings;
sad she is seven so few moments more,
a dancer balleting inevitably towards

her later days with some other
largely unworthy clown.

Promise of Rain

For Jim Thomas, (1930-2009)

I give my varied colored flowers water from the hose
so they won't wilt or forget to flower at all.

It seems to work, at times they almost glow
when they receive that wet reprieve from drought.

Rain forecast often doesn't show
or comes in lesser numbers than foretold.

So I go out again and water more to bless
their lives with what sunny skies withhold.

I'm not a gardener, I don't devote hours
to weed or mulch or prune or fertilize.

Still, I can't bear to watch the living suffer
when I have what they need in sure supply.

Sometimes I hold the hose above my head so flowers
won't suspect these raindrops aren't from heaven.

It's just me with easy patience and a hose
showering them with what caring can propose.

Physical Therapy

The petite young blonde assigned to guide
me through exercises for relief of my shoulder
pain has cold hands, but a well-trained friendliness
I believe she mostly means.

I could be embarrassed by how much stronger
she is, could fit the bill of the old guy, who
brags about how far he could once throw a football
or get grumpier still and say, "Let's wait 'til you're 61,"

but of course I won't be around to see how that works out.
A right "shoulder impingement" is hardly unbearable,
shooting pain only when I reach too far or long
for something over my head, or behind my back,

and with my family's history (three siblings
have already beaten cancer; one has not),
I complain though most would agree I can't.
Even now my younger brother, prostate cancer

gone, has three worse ailments than my single woe.
My mother-in-law has her own cancer battle,
unfair to pick one with an eighty-two-year- old
but she's still fighting. My nephew will lose

his stomach in a few days, will hope it takes
its cancer with it. I was aware long before
I met 60 that aging means debilitation, loss;
I've already been a regular, with regular lapses

visiting nursing homes, in vain efforts to cheer
any of us up. I still have two children at home,
though, and another two out of the house
who might miss me even more than they imagine.

Beyond blood, for as long as I keep my job
as a teacher, some young people will have to accept
me as mattering, at least for a term, and those
terms are still acceptable to me, since I'm certain

I can live with the pain, or better still,
avoid it almost entirely, if I remember
evermore not to reach too far above
or for anything behind.

Acknowledgments

"After Zoraida Martínez Saved Me from Divine Word Seminary," *Kansas City Voices*

"Stay-at-Home Dad," *Steam Ticket*

"Break-In," *Nomad's Choir*

"Birthday Present," *Now, Here, Nowhere*

"Marilyn Meshak," *Concho River Review*

"After Singing All Night for Twenty Bucks and a Bagel," *Diverse Voices Quarterly*

"Dancing with a Dutch Girl," *Fennel Stalk*

"After Driving to See Sylvia in Nebraska," *Botticelli Literary Magazine*

"Unsettled," *Java Snob Review*

"After December 25th," *The Blue Pen*

"What Cannot Be Feigned," *The Meadow*

"No Competition," *Homestead Review*

"Playground," *Pearl*

"After Math," *Oklahoma Review*

"After Realizing I Didn't Have Enough Money," *Oklahoma Review*

"After Finding Those Cavalcanti Poems, *Italian Americana*

"Bonifacio Payaso," *The Potomac*

"Physical Therapy," *Cacti Fur*

About the Author

Joe Benevento received a B.A. degree from NYU in English and Spanish (magna cum laude, Phi Beta Kappa), an M.A. in English from Ohio State and a Ph.D. in English from Michigan State. Benevento is Professor of English at Truman State U, where he teaches creative writing, American literature, (including Latino/Latina and Latin American lit. in translation) and Young Adult Literature and Mystery. He is the longtime, co-editor of the *Green Hills Literary Lantern*.

About the Press

Unsolicited Press was founded in 2012 and is currently based in Portland, Oregon. The team produces phenomenal poetry, fiction, and creative nonfiction. Learn more at www.unsolicitedpress.com

CPSIA information can be obtained
at www.ICGtesting.com
Printed in the USA
BVHW031658130319
542574BV00001B/91/P